Introduction

Delve into the fasc  gical traits for Dogs!

Don't fret if you don day! Pets often mirror their owners, so check out their owner's sign, or simply enjoy exploring the traits of each zodiac sign to find the best match for your furry friend.

This book is a light-hearted guide to understanding your furry friend through the lens of astrology. You might even have a laugh looking up your friends in this book! Guaranteed to bring a smile.

This book is dedicated to
my dog Toulouse who
lived to please me.
A loving Libra.

And to
Winslow, my Pisces dog.
Never a dull moment
with him.

Contents

THE ARIES DOG 2
THE TAURUS DOG 4
THE GEMINI DOG 6
THE CANCER DOG 8
THE LEO DOG 10
THE VIRGO DOG 12
THE LIBRA DOG 14
THE SCORPIO DOG 16
THE SAGITTARIUS DOG 18
THE CAPRICORN DOG 20
THE AQUARIUS DOG 22
THE PISCES DOG 24
ABOUT ME 25

The Aries Dog

THE ARIES DOG

Born Between March 20th to April 19th

A Fire Sign
Ruling Planet – Mars

ARIES DOG IS PERFECT IN EVERY WAY.
At least they think they are!

ARIES PUPPY IS FEARLESS, BOLDLY EXPLORING THEIR EVER-WIDENING ENVIRONMENT.
Even areas in the home that you wanted off limits to them.
AT AN EARLY AGE THEY WILL SHOW A HIGH ENERGY DRIVE AND AN ASSERTIVE NATURE.
They will not only have an interest in the doggy toys you have so lovingly given them but also your shoes, pillows, and other furnishings in the home. Plus, the cat if you have one.
ARIES DOG SEES EVERYTHING IN TERMS OF HIS!
Including you, the house and back garden. ARIES DOG has an impatient nature that will come out at feeding time and when you get ready for the routine walk.
THE ARIES DOG WANTS IT NOW!
YOU MUST START TRAINING AS EARLY AS POSSIBLE.
Even as an ARIES PUPPY they are head strong, have a will of their own. They are adventurous, willing to go anywhere with you or take off on their own without you. Depending on how well you have trained them, they can be a dog that you can be proud of.
ARIES DOG LOVES PRAISE AND ATTENTION FROM YOU, OFTEN!
Whether your ARIES DOG is of a large sized breed or a smaller breed, they will have the courage to think they can handle anything and any size dog.
ARIES DOG LIVES TO TAKE CHARGE, "THE ALPHA DOG."
A RISK-TAKING, LEADER OF THE PACK.
A FEARLESS LIVE WIRE WITH HIGH ENERGY, DRIVE AND INSTANT ACTION IF THIS DOG SENSES IT IS NEEDED.

GREAT CAREERS FOR AN ARIES DOG.
A police dog –They are always ready for action.
Working for the Airlines in security –They do not back down.
Guard dog- To protect, no problem.
Military dog.

The Taurus Dog

THE TAURUS DOG

Born Between April 19th to May 20th   An Earth Sign
                                        Ruling Planet – Venus

TAURUS DOG IS ALL ABOUT "I HAVE".
Life is about their possessions.

TAURUS PUPPY IS WARM HEARTED AND GENTLE.
They want you to pet and hug them as much as possible. That is why they will keep you up at night crying. TAURUS DOG loves getting toys, the more the better. They will collect all their toys and play for hours. Make sure TAURUS DOG has enough toys, or they will be in search of things to make their toys, adding to their collection, which will no longer be yours. So, if you cannot find that little something, check out TAURUS DOG's toys.

TAURUS DOG BED MUST BE THE TOP OF THE LINE IN COMFORT, PLENTY OF ROOM TO ADD TOYS AND BE PLEASING TO LOOK AT.
TAURUS DOG will know when the dog bed is not the best buy, and you will know because it will be chewed to bits! TAURUS DOG likes to be groomed often. Looking good is important to them no matter what size they are.

TAURUS DOGS WILL NOT BE RUSHED.
Do not think you can take them out for a quick walk in the evenings, think again!

JEALOUSY MAY BE A PROBLEM.
They will not want to share their toys with other dogs or cats. They cherish their human family and do not like to share them either!

TAURUS DOG IS SET IN THEIR WAYS.
Changes can be unsettling to them. Happiness is being at home. No new adventures for them.

TAURUS DOG NEEDS TO BE SURROUNDED BY THEIR STUFF.
They will not even like it if you place their bed in a new area, they will just pull it back to where it was. TAURUS DOG never gives up, is all determination and more than a little stubborn.

TAURUS DOG IS SOOTHING.
Their energy can relax the most uptight, high-strung people just by being in the same space or on their lap.

NO CAREER FOR THIS DOG.
TAURUS DOG is the stay-at-home type.

The Gemini Dog

THE GEMINI DOG

Born Between May 20th to June 21st			An Air Sign
						Ruling Planet – Mercury

GEMINI DOG IS "I THINK", "I COMMUNICATE".
This is what Gemini does best.

GEMINI DOG, THE ESCAPE ARTIST.
GEMINI DOG thinks its way out of things and places that they do not want to be in, especially if alone. They start their escape techniques as a puppy and build up from there. This is due to their tremendous curiosity and the desire not to be alone. You may start the nighttime with the puppy nicely tucked in the crate or room with everything a puppy will need for bedtime. It will not take long before you wake up to a cold nose on your face. You might as well bring their dog bed into your bedroom or a dog blanket for the bottom of the bed. You will never win.

FORGET ABOUT TRAINING.
Send GEMINI DOG away for that. They can easily be side tracked during training. Expect the unexpected from this dog. Tough to keep up with this restless, inquisitive GEMINI DOG.

CONSTANTLY ON THE GO AND VOCAL ABOUT IT.
Because of their strong curious nature, they are clever and quick to learn the things you do not want them to do.

GEMINI DOG LOVES SOCIALIZING.
They love being around people and other pets like dogs, cats, parrots, etc. Not so much fish! Unless they can eat them! GEMINI DOG will not tolerate being alone which means it is not a good idea to leave GEMINI DOG alone in your home. If you leave this dog loose or even in a crate, be prepared to find complete chaos waiting for you and a loving greeting at the door. It is best to take GEMINI DOG to work with you or leave at DOGGY DAY CARE. This will be heaven for GEMINI DOG as they love making friends.

GEMINI IS THE SIGN OF THE TWINS.
You will discover you have two dogs in one and will soon know which one you are dealing with, NAUGHTY or GOOD DOG!

HIGHLY ADAPTABLE TO CHANGING CONDITIONS.
Anything is possible for the GEMINI DOG.

GREAT CAREERS FOR A GEMINI DOG.
Your permanent Sidekick
Agility Competition sport – Loves obstacles

The Cancer Dog

THE CANCER DOG

Born Between June 21st to July 22nd   A Water Sign
                                             Ruling Planet – Moon

CANCER DOG IS "I FEEL".
Life is about nurturing, caring, and empathy.
CANCER DOG NEEDS HUGS TO FEEL YOU TRULY CARE ABOUT THEM.
After all, their life is about taking care of the family they belong to and EATING. As a puppy, you will notice straight away that they eat too fast and get into any food within reach. Often having an upset tummy which leads to cleaning up as it will be coming out both ends. This stomach problem can continue into adulthood.
CANCER DOG OFTEN ACT LIKE THEY KNOW WHAT IS BEST FOR YOU AND THE FAMILY.
The family may not even notice how controlling the CANCER DOG is. This DOG is happy to have the responsibility of watching over the family. Loving that warm, cosy feeling that comes from being with their human family and keeping them safe.
CANCER DOG IS IN YOUR FACE IF YOU ARE SAD OR CRYING. IF IT WERE POSSIBLE, THEY WOULD BRING YOU A TISSUE.
CANCER DOG can be overly sensitive to small slights, getting upset and pouting while lying on the mat in front of the door. Knowing you will be sure to see them or trip over them!
CANCER DOG BELIEVES IN THE IMPORTANCE OF FAMILY.
If there is a toddler in the family, CANCER DOG will be on the alert to pull them out of trouble by the seat of their nappy. CANCER DOG will especially follow small children if they are walking around with food. Ready for any morsel that falls from them or what the child may want to share. Best for you and the dog to put CANCER DOG on a diet. This makes them moody and quick to notice if food falls to the floor.
AFTER YOUR HOLIDAY AWAY AND PICKING UP THE DOG FROM THE KENNEL, IT WILL TAKE DAYS BEFORE SETTLING BACK INTO BEING HOME. "That is the Dog, not you!" The best thing to do when you go on vacation is to get someone to pet sit at your home. This way you will have a much happier CANCER DOG and less tummy upsets to clean up.

GREAT CAREERS FOR CANCER DOGS.
Nanny- Great with babies and children.
Also love being home.

The Leo Dog

THE LEO DOG

Born Between July 21st to August 22nd

A Fire Sign
Ruling Planet – Sun

LEO DOG IS "FUN-LOVING".
Does things on a Grand Scale, outgoing with plenty of Drama!
AS A LEO PUPPY, THEY WILL FIND OUT RIGHT AWAY WHAT BRINGS THEM PLENTY OF ATTENTION.
So that is what they will continue to do. Be careful with your reactions or they will have some bad habits that will be difficult to break.
LEO DOG NEEDS CONSTANT ATTENTION, GOOD OR BAD.
Such as humping their teddy bear or stuffed animal in front of company. They really are just showing you how happy they are having visitors to show off too. That seems to always bring attention of a kind!
LEO DOG LIKES TO BE WHERE THE ACTION IS AND THE ATTENTION ON THEM.
They like to be on the go and looking good. They like to be noticed!
LEO DOG LOVES TO BE PAMPERED.
This dog is not your stay-at-home dog and wants to socialize more. Needs people whenever possible for that badly needed attention. Showing off is everything, so be sure LEO DOG is well trained. Otherwise, you are in for huge problems.
LEO DOG WILL WEAR YOU OUT UNLESS YOU ARE FULL OF OUTGOING ENERGY, AS WELL.
This dog loves to travel, new people (all people), new places, and plenty of attention.
LEO DOG WANTS TO BE SHOWERED WITH ADMIRATION AND GIFTS.
They are showy, wanting centre stage, as they are ruled by the sun sign.
AN ATTENTION-GETTER WHEREVER THEY GO AND WITH WHAT THEY DO.
If left on their own for too long and too often you will not have much of a dog with any kind of spirit. It can become sickly and depressed.

GREAT CAREERS FOR A LEO DOG.
A show dog – Any level of show will do.
A performing dog – In the circus or movies.

The Virgo Dog

THE VIRGO DOG

Born Between August 22nd to September 22nd.   An Earth Sign
Ruling Planet - Mercury

VIRGO DOG IS "A WORRIER".
This sensitivity makes for an alert strong caring dog.

VIRGO DOG IS DOWN-TO-EARTH, SENSIBLE, AND DEPENDABLE.
An even mild dog. Shows No uncontrolled excitement. As a VIRGO PUPPY, they will get on better if there is routine in their life. Will appear serious and less playful than other puppies. VIRGO PUPPY will be incredibly interested in the detail around their living space. Do not worry if this dog is not that playful.

VIRGO PUPPY JUST WANTS TO KNOW WHAT THEY HAVE GOT THEMSELVES INTO!
VIRGO DOG must know what you expect of them as they are cautious.
Not only that they will continue staring at you until they understand what you want. "THEY STAY FOCUSED."

WHEN GREETING YOU AS YOU ARRIVE HOME.
The greeting will feel more like a handshake. None of that over excitement of jumping all over you. VIRGO DOG feels there is no need for that, you both know you love each other.

VIRGO DOG MAY STAND CLOSE TO GET THAT PAT ON THE HEAD.
They will never lose the bones they have buried in the garden. VIRGO DOG knows where each and every bone or toy is buried!

VIRGO DOG LIVES TO BE OF SERVICE TO YOU, AN EASY-GOING DOG.
Can wait hours watching and waiting for your attention. Focusing only on you. When VIRGO DOG does have you to themselves, they are in heaven, but they will not show it.

NO TASK IS TOO LARGE OR SMALL FOR THEM.
VIRGO DOG has an eye for detail and lives to care for their human. Accommodating to your every wish. Which can feel too good to be true or suffocating. Loves to be of use to people, essential to their wellbeing.

HAS NO INTEREST IN OTHER PETS, INDIFFERENT TO THEM.

GREAT CAREERS FOR VIRGO DOG.
A Guide Dog – Help people with sight loss.
Medical Detection Dog.
Dog care assistants- For the Autistic or people with extreme anxiety.

The Libra Dog

THE LIBRA DOG

Born Between September 22nd to October 22nd   An Air Sign
                                                          Ruling Planet – Venus

LIBRA DOG "LIVES TO PLEASE".
They focus on doing what makes you happy.

LIBRA DOG CAN BE POSSESSIVE:
They want to be the only one that matters in your life, will often remind you of this by never leaving you alone. They will always be under foot or lying on your feet.

LIBRA DOG AS A PUPPY WILL BE PLAYFUL AND LOVING.
Easy to land up with a wet face from their loving nature. It will seem like your puppy is always happy, which it is!

LIBRA DOG WANTS TO BE TOLD WHAT TO DO. THEY LIVE FOR YOUR ATTENTION AND WAIT FOR YOUR COMMAND.
Which makes them highly cooperative. If you are not around, you have a lazy dog that will find cosy places to sleep. Otherwise, they are indecisive as to what they should do.

LIBRA DOG NEEDS A WELL-BALANCED HOME.
This dog tends to be overly sensitive, it will show this stress from the tip of its nose, through its eyes, down to the end of their tail and a lack of tail wagging. For example, if a puppy accidentally knocks over its food plate during mealtime, it can lead to a fear of that object in some puppies. This could lead to a fear of plates in the future, making it hesitant to eat from them. A dog bowl might be a more suitable option, unless that also causes distress.

LIBRA DOGS ARE HAPPY DOGS IN GENERAL.
Happiest if they have a well-balanced life. Any cruelty to LIBRA DOG will kill their spirit. "They are a lover not a fighter".

LIBRA DOG IS FUSSY ABOUT THEIR FOOD:
You will notice they only like the best. If not happy, which is unusual, they will overeat if they are able too. They like the best of most things, especially if it makes them look good. For example, a bright new collar.

LIBRA DOG BELIEVES "TOO MUCH IS A GOOD THING!" LIBRA DOG LIKES LOOKING GOOD, AND THEY KNOW WHEN THEY DO!
The groomer is their friend. They know they are made to look good! You can read "Look at me!" on their sweet doggy faces.
NOTHING BETTER THAN SHOWING OFF.

GREAT CAREER FOR A LIBRA DOG.
Being shown in the dog shows.

The Scorpio Dog

THE SCORPIO DOG

Born Between October 22nd to November 22nd A water Sign
                                                         Ruling Planet – Pluto

SCORPIO DOG HAS "PIERCING EYES" WITH "PHYSICAL STAMINA".
Determination is one sign of MAJOR STRENGTHS.
SCORPIO DOG IS FULL OF SURPRISES, GOOD OR BAD.
This dog also has a stubborn side, you first notice it in their puppy stage of life. You may think at first the SCORPIO PUPPY is not too bright. The thing is they have sized you up and know just what they can get away with.
THERE ARE TIMES YOU GET THE FEELING THAT SCORPIO DOG IS "PSYCHIC".
Like knowing what you wanted before you even asked, or behaving in a way that perfectly aligned with your unspoken desires, this feels almost magical! Sometimes it can be a little spooky around SCORPIO DOG.
IT IS THOSE PIERCING EYES.
SCORPIO DOG has such strong powers of observation, intuition, and the ability to sense what is needed to be done. This dog is emotionally deep and once they give you their loyalty, you have it for the lifetime of the dog. SCORPIO DOG is the one that sees you off at the train station and is there when you return, waiting as long as it takes. If for some reason, you cannot or do not return, this dog will be waiting for you for the rest of its life, there at the station.
"ON THE OTHER HAND", SCORPIO DOG IS REVENGEFUL.
Once they get even, all is back to being fine. For example, you start to neglect this dog. SCORPIO DOG will know what your favourite object in the house is or maybe your favourite chair. It will wait until the time is right and chew that object or chair to bits and maybe add some pee!
VENGEANCE IS THEIRS.
SCORPIO DOG has a magnetic energy that draws people to them. It has the power to mesmerize almost anyone with a single look. It is like they know who and what you are.
THERE IS JUST SOMETHING FASCINATING ABOUT THE SCORPIO DOG.

GREAT CAREER FOR SCORPIO DOGS.
A Secret Agent.

The Sagittarius Dog

THE SAGITTARIUS DOG

Born between November 22nd to December 21st A Fire Sign
Ruling Planet – Jupiter

SAGITTARIUS DOG IS "ADVENTURESOME".
A freedom loving spirit who is forever on the go.
SAGITTARIUS DOG'S PASSION IS FREEDOM AND MORE FREEDOM.
As long as the dog is travelling or working, SAGITTARIUS DOG is in their "HAPPY PLACE".
SAGITTARIUS DOG IS A HIGH ENERGY RESTLESS DOG THAT NEEDS TO BE KEPT BUSY THROUGHOUT THE DAY.
If you have a laid-back somewhat quiet stay at home family life, then you and your family will be miserable living with this dog. So will your neighbours as this is not a dog that will stay on their own property. SAGITTARIUS DOG must check out everyone's garden. The more gardens to see the happier the dog, and the more miserable you are! SAGITTARIUS DOG can be impulsive with non-stop energy, looking for fascinating things to do.
FOREVER ON THE GO. SAGITTARIUS DOG IS GENTLE AND UPBEAT.
Normally enthusiastic and spreading good cheer by jumping up on to people to show how pleased it is to meet them. A response that will be hard to train them not to do. This is how they express their happiness.
SAGITTARIUS DOG IS GENERALLY FRIENDLY AND OUTGOING.
Does not do well with children as SAGITTARIUS DOG tends to knock or trip them over. Cats are not happy with them either. SAGITTARIUS DOG is intelligent and learns fast. Except not to jump up on people and cats.
SAGITTARIUS DOG HAS A GREAT IMAGINATION.
If left alone for too long, you will be surprised how fast this DOG can make changes in your home. SAGITTARIUS DOG is really an outdoor type of dog exploring the wilds of nature. Unless it is a tiny dog that sees the world from a carrier pouch all day long. That is okay too. Either way, "This is the life"!
SAGITTARIUS DOG IS THE ALPHA DOG LEADING THE PACK INTO MISCHIEF, A BORN TEACHER.

GREAT CAREERS FOR A SAGITTARIUS DOG.
Outdoor career- Sniffing out Truffles.
Door Greeter
Ship Mascot

The Capricorn Dog

THE CAPRICORN DOG

Born between December 21st to January 20th   An Earth Sign
Ruling Planet – Saturn

CAPRICORN DOG IS A "LEARN-BY-DOING" SIGN.
Born with the determination to achieve.
CAPRICORN DOG IS ACTION-ORIENTED.
This dog is serious, not playful unless they are learning something important. Not interested in playing or going after a ball. That is below them. They have the drive and determination to be "TOP DOG".
CAPRICORN DOG LIVES FOR RECOGNITION.
CAPRICORN PUPPY starts out acting like a much older dog.
THIS DOG HAS AN OLD SOUL.
CAPRICORN PUPPY will think and plan before acting and approach each task with organized action. The better training you have for this dog, the more excellent the dog will be with people or the jobs they are trained to do.
CAPRICORN DOG IS RESERVED.
Strong sense of duty to the owner and family. No matter the size of the dog, CAPRICORN DOG will forever have that look of dignity, strength and wisdom. Sometimes making him look unapproachable. If you are into cuddly, playful and easy-going dogs, you will not find it in a CAPRICORN DOG "KEEP LOOKING!" CAPRICORN DOG will have a way of making you feel that you are the stupid one. It is the seriousness that a CAPRICORN DOG has.
CAPRICORN DOG HAS AN EXCELLENT MEMORY.
So be careful how you treat them. You do not wish to wake up in the morning having this dog staring down at you with that certain look in their eyes. Otherwise, CAPRICORN DOG is great to have around.
YOU FOREVER KNOW WHERE YOU STAND WITH CAPRICORN DOG.
This is the dog that can be trusted home alone, or with children and other pets.
CAPRICORN DOG LOVES CHILDREN.
This is the dog that will be pulling the lost child by its nappy home or to a safe place.
RULES ARE PART OF CAPRICORN DOG'S LIFE, NEVER BREAKS THEM.

GREAT CAREERS FOR A CAPRICORN DOG.
Police Dog- Tracking missing children.
Helping Santa to make children happy.

The Aquarius Dog

THE AQUARIUS DOG

Born Between January 20th to February 19th   An Air Sign
                                                Ruling Planet – Uranus

AQUARIUS DOG HAS A REBELLIOUS NATURE.
Hard to predict what AQUARIUS DOG will do next, "UNIQUE".

AQUARIUS PUPPY WILL COME ACROSS DETACHED TOWARDS YOU.
Not much for showing affection, more aloof and impersonal. This will continue into adulthood. So do not wait for that cuddle, jumping up on you, and licking your face, action.

AQUARIUS DOG SHOWS ITS LOVE THROUGH LOYALTY.

THIS DOG IS INTELLIGENT, WITH UNIQUE CHARACTERISTICS.
This dog has a type of magnetism that many would find fascinating.

AQUARIUS DOG IS FRIENDLY AND EXPRESSES A GENTLE, GENUINE INTEREST IN PEOPLE.
They are most happy when in the company of other dogs. They cannot wait for trips to the DOG PARK, to see all their friends. Doggy Day Care and Dog Walking Groups make them just as happy.

AQUARIUS DOG IS DETERMINED AND STUBBORN.
Their determination can be relentless when in pursuit of a goal. Like finding that bone that was buried weeks ago.

AQUARIUS DOG COMES ALIVE WHEN NEAR A BODY OF WATER.
Having that stubbornness, it will be more than difficult to get the AQUARIUS DOG out of the water and on your way. Even a small dog will wiggle its way out of your arms.

AQUARIUS DOG LIVES IN THE FUTURE.
Forever ahead of itself in thinking. Hard to predict what AQUARIUS DOG will do next. If you are not a person that can go with the flow of things, this dog will drive you crazy!

AQUARIUS DOG MAKES FRIENDS EASILY WITH OTHER PETS IN THE HOUSEHOLD.
Those other pets can be all kinds of animals or birds. They love to make friends with the other dogs, cats, parrots, hamsters or whatever. Rather, they just love to make friends. It is when this dog starts bringing them home that it becomes a problem for YOU! AQUARIUS DOG is under the symbol of the HUMANITARIAN.

GREAT CAREERS FOR AQUARIUS DOG.
Coast Guard Mascot.
Lifeguard assistant.

The Pisces Dog

THE PISCES DOG

Born Between February 19th to March 20th   A Water Sign
                                                                                    Ruling Planet – Neptune

PISCES DOG IS VERY CONCERNED ABOUT DOING THE RIGHT THING.
They are highly sensitive and trusting.

PISCES PUPPY IS EASY-GOING.
Will enjoy any fun thing you would like to do. They will follow right along. PISCES DOG loves being around people, especially at parties. They will even wear the party hat. Also good at stealing the attention from the person who the party is for.

HAS A SENSE OF HUMOR.
PISCES DOG will do something that it knows is wrong and then turn around to make sure you have seen it, with what looks like a smile on their face. PISCES DOG easily picks up the vibrations of people, places, and things. A psychic sensitivity, with a STRONG SIXTH SENSE. They will have a way to express these feelings to you, knows when there is danger around or someone is hurt, or a fun place to be in!

JUST LISTEN, YOUR PISCES DOG KNOWS WHAT IS GOING ON.
They are so open to the energy around them and convey it to you. PISCES DOG can adapt to changing circumstances to fit in anywhere and will get on great with other pets. They can sense what other animals are feeling, wanting to help if needed. That is why a PISCES DOG makes a great DOG to have when you are caring for other pets.

PISCES DOG WILL TAKEOVER TO ASSIST THE PETS YOU ARE CARING FOR.
An example, when I was caring for a blind dog, and would take this blind dog out. The PISCES DOG would get right next to this dog with his body guiding the blind dog. It was touching to see this.

PISCES DOG IS A CHARMER, A TRUE LOVER OF PEOPLE.
Has a way to put people at ease. Friendly and generates enthusiasm. PISCES DOG often has a friend dog of the opposite sex that he or she likes to hang around with.

GREAT CAREERS FOR A PISCES DOG.
An assistant Pet Sitter.
A travelling companion.
A Party Partner.

ABOUT ME

Betty-Ann Beaulieu – A Lover of Animals.

Growing up in the United States, I had a deep fondness for animals. My childhood was filled with impromptu wildlife rescues, from birds that had fallen from their nests to frogs and turtles seeking refuge. While my parents weren't always enthusiastic about my newfound "pets," my passion for animal care was undeniable.

Raised by an English mother who instilled in me a strong sense of British culture, I attended Salisbury College of Art and Design in England, where I honed my skills in Graphic Art, Photography, Display, and Drawing. Upon returning to the United States, I embarked on a career in the creative field, working as a Graphic Artist in advertising and later as a Display Artist for renowned department stores.

In 2005, I relocated to Bainbridge Island near Seattle, Washington, where I spent over a decade providing loving care to pets through my pet-sitting services. This rewarding experience further deepened my connection with animals. I have also dedicated time to expanding my understanding of animal communication through studies at the Reno, Nevada Psychic Institute.

Currently, I reside in North Wales, UK, where I pursue my passion for creativity as a freelance artist, creating my own graphics and illustrations alongside my writing

Layout and illustrations by Betty-Ann Beaulieu
Edited by Adesope Badejo

Printed in Great Britain
by Amazon